PRAISE FOR ᵁHE LIES WE WEAVE...

"Grace Reynolds once again uses her keyboard as a spinneret to weave a collection of dark poetry like no other. Themes of girlhood, womanhood and motherhood collide, exploring all the ways that the female form is consumed in life as well as in death. Fans of dark prose will enjoy this beautifully written, highly personal poetry collection that poses the question of why we choose to believe the lies we tell ourselves about ourselves, and empowers us to break the cycle."
—Wendy Dalrymple, author of WHITE IBIS

"THE LIES WE WEAVE is an unflinching look into the darkness and the stories you tell yourself to survive it. This book is a dark song, a paean to mental health, motherhood, and the beautiful grotesque. Grace R. Reynolds is one of the best horror poets working in the genre today."
—Jessica Drake-Thomas, author of BURIALS and BAD OMENS

"In her darkly gorgeous new book, Grace Reynolds has crafted a poetry collection that is both feminist and feminine. Beautiful and bloody, aching and viscerally affecting, Reynolds skillfully carves her words into our flesh—this is all of us, each struggle to be seen and to hide, to reclaim our bodies and also create ourselves anew."
—Laurel Hightower, author of CROSSROADS and BELOW

"As delightful as it is devastating, THE LIES WE WEAVE showcases Grace R. Reynolds' skill with dark poetry and prose in examining motherhood as an excision, contagion, and

revelation while exploring the gorgeous and gory nature of femininity."
—Jessica McHugh, Bram Stoker Award-nominated author of A COMPLEX ACCIDENT OF LIFE

"THE LIES WE WEAVE is breathtakingly beautiful and hauntingly visceral. You cannot read this collection without feeling it move beneath the surface of your skin. Reynolds has constructed an intricate, intimate exploration of womanhood and the self that is earthy, cosmic and utterly transfixing."
—Emily Verona, Bram Stoker Award-nominated author

The Lies

We Weave

Poetry and Prose
Written by Grace R. Reynolds

Curious Corvid
PUBLISHING

For the mothers

and the young women we used to be.

We are enough.

We have always been enough.

INTRODUCTION

Melancholy (adjective)

1. suggestive or expressive of sadness, depression of mind or spirit.

2. depressed in the spirits: DEJECTED. SAD.

Depravity (noun)

1. a corrupt act or practice

2. the quality or state of being corrupt, evil, or perverted: the quality of being depraved.

I think about these two words a lot and often muse over their applicability to my person. The first definition I know to be an irrefutable truth. For as long as I can remember, I have been a person who has walked with an inexplicable pervasive sadness. I don't necessarily mind it, but there are times when it manifests into a more sinister form of dejection. Like black bile, it seeps from my spirit.

In these moments, my mind tells me horrible things about myself. The depravity of my existence: something to apologize for or acknowledge or accept. Are they lies, or are they complex, unspoken truths that crawl under my skin? Part of me knows that many of my intrusive thoughts are not true, but another part is unsure. What is real? What isn't?

I never wanted to write about some of the themes in this book. I feared myself to be too vulnerable or perhaps not vulnerable enough. One of the beautiful things about poetry is that a writer can give themselves permission to leave shallow waters and explore the depths of their emotions at their own pace, and so that is what I have chosen to do.

I permitted myself to confront the parts of me that I feared— the shadow figures lurking in my mind's corners. The ones that I chose to ignore, and instead told myself, "there's no one there; my monsters are not real."

In this collection, I challenged myself to confront my pain. Where could it be pruned? Where did I need to pull it out from the root? Who was I doing this for? If not for myself, could I not examine my feelings for the sake of my children?

I explored different facets of my life that most often influence my person, and as I am a mother, the theme of motherhood came up repeatedly. From that, I examined my journey into womanhood and motherhood, and somehow came out the other side stronger for it.

This book, however, is no longer mine and belongs to you now, dear reader. As you journey through these pages, I want you to consider the lies, no matter how small or large, you tell yourself every day that break your heart in a million ways. I want you to confront your depravity. Think about the knives you gave someone else to carve up your skin and the scars you felt the need to hide.

Why is it we go on when there is so much pain? Are you, too, depraved? How much of yourself are you willing to look at in the mirror so you can see yourself – *all of yourself.*

"Don't ever let your grief or anger fester inside of you, for it will eat you alive. Let it die, and let it rise."

Sincerely,

Grace R. Reynolds

CONTENT WARNING

The following book contains themes and imagery of graphic violence, sexual assault, gore, anxiety, depression, self-harm, prenatal, perinatal, and neonatal care.

TABLE OF CONTENTS

PRELUDE

DIMENSIONS OF TRUTH

I do not recall my last breath,

but I remember everything after.

I remember the inky blackness of space,

how my soul hurtled towards cosmic clusters

of nebulae reaching towards the heavens, and I

a newborn, wrapped in the creamy coating

of vernix caseosa searching for sound in my lungs

to scream for my mother's breast.

An inherit knowing that I was 'home.'

How long I waded in the pools of eternity

I do not know, but they welcomed me

into their billowing embrace and held my essence

as I looked into the yawning pathways of the universe.

I more than peered into those pathways.

I yearned to fall into them.

I wanted to know what else was out there,

voyage into the unknown, and maybe I would see

other worlds, planes of existence where humans,

or other species, existed in harmony: where war

did not ravage its inhabitants, where utopia

existed.

I did not realize the other side would show me

all the ramifications of my existence.

The consequences of my actions,

all the dimensions of truth.

My truth.

The tug of the void called to me.

I heard the expansion of the universe droning,

humming, urging me to dive

into

            its

                    depths.

How very wrong was I

to dive.

I hesitated and wondered what would happen

if I disturbed the safety of my holding pattern

in the obsidian lake I floated in, but still

I

      reached

           over

                the

                    edge.

Ripples of starlight

ebbed around me, the void drew nearer,

and the bitter chill of space snapped

at my ethereal form.

The gaping maw of the abyss

opened wide, and every nerve in my body

reverberated in retaliation, but I had to know.

I had to know.

I stretched my body further, until finally I was

falling

    straight

        into

           the

               chasm.

The nothingness consumed me in an instant,

swallowed me whole, the cold wrapped

and squeezed my body until

I thought my lungs would burst.

Did I even have lungs in this form?

Inescapable dread crawled across

my skin, and I knew this was it.

This was the end.

I had ventured too far into the darkness.

VERMICULUS

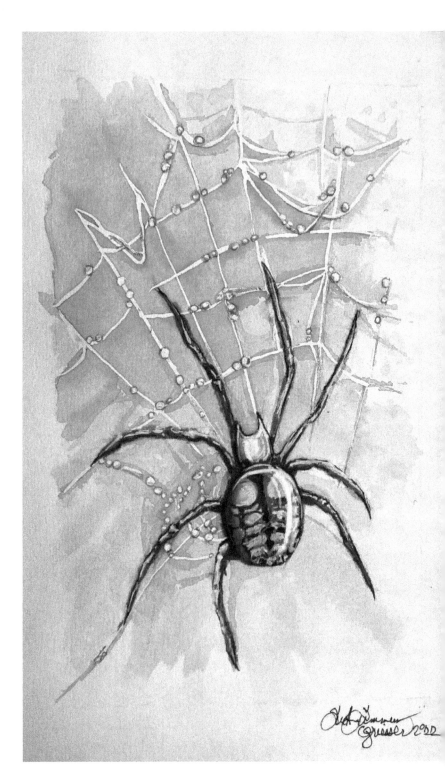

THE WEAVER

It wasn't supposed to be this way.

The words reverberated through my brain

over and over as the orb weaver dangled

in front of me like she had done this before.

"I will eat you alive" she said

　　　　　　　　　"I am already dead inside" I replied

Naivety pendulous, survival incredulous,

conflagrated trust, a diamond in the rough,

I tried to bear its weight, the incremental pressure,

displeasure of existence, but still

　　　　　　　　　"It wasn't supposed to be this way."

"I have already laid my eggs."

Impregnation, dissident of my damnation,

fleeting opportunity, instinctual mutiny,

her ambition planted in the hard roof of my palate.

I must be careful not to disturb them

with my tongue.

Shallow

How long will you hold

      me under shallow waters

           just to watch me drown?

Sanctity of A Hiding Place

The shadows hold close the secrets we keep, memories that are sticky— lacquered in layers of dust, termites, and mouse hair on shelves where tchotchkes bore silent witness,

Where our pain is wrought on walls underneath coats of paint, covering the places our nail beds scratched and bled, markings we hoped would surface as evidence, proving our presence,

Where our screams were muted by basement wood paneling, shag carpets, and neighbors who rolled over in their beds,

Where more of us died than lived, where the survivors learned the sanctity of staying hid.

Monsoon Season

I daydream,

under wet canopies, droplets roll

off the leaves, and somehow,

I tell myself, "this is rain."

I lay here, choking

on the copper tang, and wonder

if I have forgotten how to swim

or if I have already chosen

to abandon the notion of a life raft,

a vessel of hope, ready to carry me

away from a pain I refuse

to name.

A Mother's Love

Mother's love is a haunted room,

brimming with secrets, it splinters

through boards like rusty nails

bent at the head, and a daughter hides

in her closet, praying the rotten wood

does not collapse beneath.

How many times has a daughter broken

her nails, digging them into the grain?

Mother's love is trapped

in sticky glue between paper

and plaster, her screams bubbling

behind the surface, and a daughter

is afraid to peel it away.

How many times has Mother cried out

her name while a daughter held her breath?

Mother's love bleeds,

it drips off glass shards,

and seeps into the floor,

and a daughter's hands are dirty,

ruddy and brown, her fingers still clasped

in prayer for a god that isn't there.

But if a god was there, then he was hiding too,

silent like the tears running down a daughter's face.

What is she supposed to do?

Mother's love drags,

it pulls her down into dark places,

spaces where her daughter cannot save her,

and how would a daughter save her

when a mother's love glints

on the edge of a razor?

GENERATIONAL FIB I

"I

would

die for

you," she says,

my lungs fight the need

to expand, one by one, they burst,

hemlock in my throat, her hands grip my neck and I choke,

blood runs from my eyes, poison oak,

my wounds suppurate

bleed, I look

at the

scars

on

her

arms.

It looks

like she has

been scratching them, too.

GENERATIONAL FIB II

In

a

corner,

backed, she is

feral, lashing out

at anything or anyone

who comes near, teeth bared,

clumps of flesh

fall from

her

mouth,

my

wounds

covered,

I draw near

and remember she

cannot see who pushed her there first.

Indiscriminate Angst

We didn't know

how sharp our nails were

until they broke skin, drew blood,

made us howl at the moon.

We didn't know

the strength of our bite

until our jaws snapped, splintered bones,

our tongues penance for the words

that could never be unspoken.

We didn't know

with every furious howl

we would forget who we were,

mauling indiscriminately,

until finally, the moon's curse wore off

and shame was all that was left

for us to carry.

WE ARE THE WICKED

We are the wicked,

spun from the charred hair

of the cursed before us, hungry

for a taste of goodness to drip

on our tongues from the tips

of our blades that beckon

to unfurl our forms

under moonlight, our sacrifice

to the old goddess in defiance of the new.

We are the wicked,

both living and dead, dragging

our stumps through the forest

leaving crimson trails for our sisters

to follow, where thickets of brambles

grow, paths where our blood still glistens

to show the way through.

I Hate Silence

I hate silence.

I hate how it feels against my skin,

a heavy blanket made of wool

laden with mites, ticks, and fleas.

It burrows through my pores

and wriggles in my capillaries.

I hate silence.

I hate how it tastes,

like oysters— chewy and bland,

a dullness that slides down my tongue.

I want to gag and regurgitate

its slimy essence.

I hate silence.

I hate how it fails to hold me

when I am weak, when my heart bleeds

on a fractured bed of femurs

buckling under the weight of heartache,

and I cannot breathe—

I hate silence.

I hate the company it brings:

the solitary "me"

alone with my thoughts

choking on misery.

INNOCENCE LOST

She always imagined the day
Death came for her would be the day
she tore the world apart.

She imagined her nails would rip
into the threads of time, curtains of black velvet
starlight, to show that she was still there, a child lost
in the magic of fairy tales, the enchantment
of fireflies, the innocence of youth.

She imagined her teeth would sink
into the meaty hearts of angels sent to carry her
to Heaven, and she would thrash until
their rib cages exploded, giving her wings to fly.

When Death came for her,
she was declawed, muzzled, and clipped.
She forgot that she was not crafted to be used,

someone else's tool, compliance whittled

from Adam's ribs.

Wit's End

I used to dream of the moths:

how their wings fluttered,

tickled my eyelashes,

how their legs pitter-pattered

across my cheeks, balmy in the glow

of a summer's end, and I let myself

drift into the nothingness

of everlasting sleep.

Sleep has never come easy for me.

Dreams twist into nightmares,

realms where I choke on the cold earth,

my body home to the mold spores

and moths crawling in the pits of my eyes,

as they feed upon the lies.

I weave them for myself like tiny threads,

 pulling at my wit's end, and

I struggle to breathe but understand.

It is only in the face of death I can see

how vulnerable our dreams are to fray.

LARVAE

EMPTY OBSCURITIES

I realized from an early age that my body is not my body. I learned that it is a morsel; a gobbet of flesh for the consumption of ver(men) to gnaw upon.

A vessel for scavengers to obscure and inhabit— a husk bulging, bloated, as the writhing dance of maggots hide false pretenses buried somewhere inside pockets of space between bone and tissue.

How strange it is to feel a sense of absence crawling under the skin like mites, their bites leaving blisters like evidence, a map to who I was, what I did, where I died, where my body was hidden.

But is it not enough that my body should rot somewhere unknown, even to me? Lost in the memories of a girl coiling her hands around a music box filled with jewelry, old coins, and baby teeth?

I'm packed away, no longer to be found. There will be no burial for me, like a wake without a body, a funeral with no grave.

THE AGONY OF EVERYTHING

Hope. Such a distant thing, like a rain cloud

prayed for when I am already drowning

in acid that boils my blood, bubbling green—

Jealousy. An unending dissatisfaction

poisons my roots, my skin is scratched raw

and weeping with blisters.

Maybe I need to be planted in a bigger pot,

placed somewhere in the sunshine,

but I've never known the firmness

of being rooted where I am planted.

The itch to break free from the mold
I have been given.

Do not water me; it is pruning I yearn for.

It is the pain that blooms under the blade

of a paring knife running under

the folds of my skin that I crave.

It is the agony of feeling

everything.

BLOOD MEAL IN THE GARDEN

I am meat—

a body, used and abused,

like a bovine laying on a table waiting

for blood to be spilled from her gullet.

Does she know why

the butcher readies himself

for the slaughter?

No, of course not, she is only a cow

as much as I am a woman struggling

to understand why man can be so cruel—

I do not remember the sound of her voice,

but I remember the screams.

Packed and sealed, a byproduct ready

to be dried for consumption.

I think of her as I admire the rose bushes

unfolding in the garden.

She is "The Buried"

Her limbs were the felled branches
spores of fungi sprouted upon,
decomposing remnants that burst red
like caps of mushrooms or antlers shedding velvet.

She is called "The Buried"—
a corpse rotting in silence. She is home
to the detritivores that salivate and masticate her
skin, home to the dross that wriggled down her
 gizzard until she was nothing more than a casting.

Who she was before does not matter,
her skeleton resembles something
much different now.

Her brain matter long decomposed,
her humors absorbed by the soil.

Did she ever have a purpose

other than fertilizing the earth?

In life, her body was never hers,

so too in death, she continued

her path to serve everything else

above herself.

QUEEN OF GROT

I chew on rotten leaves

to taste death on my tongue—

A goddess among worms,

a conqueror of none.

HOUSE OF PERTURBATION

This is my natural habitat:

a place where I am wrapped

in the woven threads of my bed

collapsing under the pressure of existence;

a place where anxiety blooms like mold spores

growing inside my chest; a place where home

feels like death.

HAGMOTH LIES

I'd

crack open

my rib cage every night,

free the hag moths and flies

fluttering inside,

a silent prayer

to feel alive;

a release

from

death

looming

behind my eyes.

Preference for Hurt

Shredded bits of skin

    float effortlessly

        down to the floor

the way all shaved things do:

    without guilt

        without weight

            just as they are.

I watch them drop,

the minced flesh of my hands,

and I should not be surprised

by my preference for hurt, yet

I am.

    "I am. I am. I am." [1]

Does my malice know no bounds?

1   *The Bell Jar*, Sylvia Plath

The Fresh Cut

Blood drips down her wrists

onto her thighs, like wilted petals—

sticky, glistening on a hot summer's

morning where the grass smells

a particular shade of green.

She never wanted to be in pain, never wanted

pervasive sadness to creep, seep into every facet

of her life, but it has, and so she sits,

a lilting stem half-broken, still craving

rays of sunshine and trickles of rain

to keep her alive, despite the distress signals

blaring from the blades.

She would rather ignore the trauma

of slicing up a living thing because

the alternative looks and smells

too good.

Goosegrass

We cleave the dying parts of ourselves—

sinew from muscle, limbs of our bodies

charred by the flames.

We leave them to waste

in fields of rot and decay

for carrion to feast upon

and pray our bones turn red.

We hunger for the living

to taste the remnants of who we were,

our names dangling like tattered flesh

from their beaks, for who are we

without our names?

Skin casings in the sun.

The hot stink of antiquity.

Bone Tea

Bone Tea.

Bitter, like me.

Steeped in the soft tissue

of marrow, spongy and soft,

cooked just right to prove a taste

that is so buttery and sweet—

something I could never truly be,

for I am but a nettle leaf,

and I am burning like

the gaping sores

inside your cheeks.

Spit Ash In My Mouth

The intimate touch of her blackened carcass,

charring and crackling, splitting embers

molten hot with despair and eternal longing.

Will you not give her

the first taste of ecstasy?

Will you not let her salamander tongue

slither across her crusted skin into your mouth?

What does it matter if she spits ash?

Her sin still feels the same.

POCKMARKED CONFESSIONS

Guilt clusters, then spreads,

irregular in pattern, always leaving

bumps and holes that mottle the soul

like pockmarked scars on skin.

Cover up is futile

when fleshy craters fester

and suppurate to the surface,

as lies often do, yet we try anyways

unaware of how our attempts

burn us further like acid, until

one day we are unfamiliar with the face

staring back at us in the mirror.

Trust Breaks, Love Leans

Somewhere between equivocation and revelation

 stands a bridge once built on trust, where

the susurrus of a river below flows into the gaping

maw of a reservoir that is neither empty, nor does it

overflow, but simply exists, like unspoken truths

that hang between parted lips, silent, their creaking

weight swinging from the end of a rope between

acknowledgment and ignorance.

Somewhere along the bridge of revelation and

equivocation, once spoken truths can

never be unheard, never be unknown, they are

forced into a hangman's knot, dropped until their

necks are crooked and limp, like bone through

muscle, forever splintering a relationship.

BASTION OF LIES

A countenance devoid of mirth,

so grim with dissatisfaction and

a heart that palpitates with

cataclysmic rage—

you study the glint of my blade.

I wonder, how does it taste?

My name in your mouth?

Have you choked on the blood

that suppurates on the nub

of the tongue I cut out?

I'd fondle your bastion of lies

were it not the muscle I most despise,

and resolve to leave it to rot

among the crows and the flies,

but it matters not, for you have already carved

your name into my bones:

Your grave marker.

Your osseous tombstone.

I Gave You This Knife

I felt everything, you know.
The burn of your blade, how it sliced
through flesh on the small of my back
where you once rested your hands.

I didn't want to believe
it was you behind me;
I didn't want to believe
I had given you the tool
to destroy me.

I didn't want
to stop you.

It was too good,
your skin brushing against mine,
even when your grip popped discs

in my spine, you yanked

and I rattled,

forever bound in chains

to you.

LINGER

I peeled you back
like a hangnail in my mind—
crusted, dead, skin flapping
in between the prints of my fingers,

the ones I used to stroke jagged edges,
so irritating, and like you, it lingers.

Were it not such a pain to pick away,
I would be rid of the discomfort,
but instead, it seems, I have chosen
an affinity for masochism of which
I'm not sure I will recover.

WISP

I felt you creeping into the marrow of my bones

when all I wanted was to be left alone,

so I took a blade and skinned away

the muscle and flesh that remembered your name.

I stripped my veins,

they sizzled and hissed,

they steamed in vain

memories of our last kiss.

I carved away the bits of my thighs,

the ones you caressed with all your lies.

I scalped my head, cut out my heart,

let my body collapse, to rot in the dark,

and when I thought I had regained control,

I felt you there stroking the wisp of my soul.

ALMOST

Your obsession

with embalming my skin

felt almost like love,

so I just laid there

and let you in.

SECRETS DRENCHED

Find me under floorboards that squeak

and creak from the insurmountable pressure

of your body on top of mine—

I know you felt my hot breath against your neck

as I struggled to stave off the touch of death.

I should have bitten your jugular,

should have scratched out your eyes,

but I could not because you crushed me,

made me obsolete like a box of memories

filled with candles, Polaroids, and panties,

but you refuse to get rid of me.

Why won't you get rid of me?

You hold onto me like a dirty secret—

a trophy, a linen napkin drenched

in menstrual blood hiding inside

the lining of your pocket waiting

to stamp your hand like a stigmata

for someone, anyone, to see—

 but first

they will smell me

Metallic and earthy,

they will feel my presence prickle

across their skin before they hear

the moans under loose boards groan,

underneath their feet is revealed the crawlspace

where you kept me.

And you'll show them your scars,

tell them you are Holy,

but I am the demon here—

I am the poltergeist.

This is *my* haunting.

You will never

be rid of me.

Let Go

Drowning in truths
too painful to swallow,
too hazy to remember,
and yet her skin remembers—

She felt the pain in her chest tighten,
leather stretched taut, still she didn't understand
why.

She had pushed the truth down,
moved out, moved forward, away
from the anger and sadness that boiled her blood,
turned her heart septic.

She had moments,
alcohol induced, panic driven numbness
that left her breathless, but she chose to move
forward, move on, let go.

So why wouldn't her body let go?

Move out.

     Move forward.

          Move on.

               Let go.

Buried Truths

Gasping for breath, I am

hollow, cottonmouth, scratching

for the surface, my screams no longer heard

six feet underground.

I buried my truth so deep it left me

breathless, like a corpse withering away

in a coffin waiting for grave robbers

to unearth who I once was,

ready to steal the trinkets I held

dear in life, what I refused

to part with in death.

Do you know what they would find

if they were to unearth me?

A skeleton, my skull a row of jagged teeth,

sharpened from the hours I tried to gnaw

my way out until I stopped breathing.

POCKETBOOK THERAPY

Trauma lives inside the body.

It rattles against rib cages

like loose change, key rings,

and shattered compact kisses

pressed against melted lipstick,

rusted paper clips,

and dried out pens.

Will you scrape

the marrow of your bones?

Will you swipe blindly

through the pain in search

of that which punctured your spirit

and stained your name?

THERE ARE HOLES EVERYWHERE

And I struggle to spackle the spaces

where I have come apart at the seams

to expose my black mold and rotten beams.

Am I worth cause to renovate?

Do I deserve the love of a fresh coat of paint?

I wonder what I would become

if someone were to share their tools with me,

to show that despite my crumbling foundation

I am still standing:

still creaking; still breathing,

and I am worth saving.

SHE CARVED HERSELF A NEW PATH

Vines curl around her flesh,

line her intestines; she burns in her new form.

Who gave her the blade

so that she could slough the muscle away?

Ruby red, her obliques shimmer under moonlight

as her skin lays in discarded ribbons.

Who will recognize the woman

that carved herself a new future?

One that was not expected, forged

in trails of entrails and blood?

Still, They Burn

I gouged out my eyes with

metal spoons, cupping them until

they made a squelching pop.

I do not need to see what I already hear.

I do not need to see the faces that look at me

with disdain as I walk past, sweat dripping from

their brows as something inside this body

makes them burn, something inside

this body that makes them feel entitled

to my worth.

They saw the gaping pits where my seafoam orbs

once were— hollowed out, and still they burned.

Will women continue to sever their limbs,

strip themselves of everything they once were,

just to avoid another day on the pyre?

I refuse to cleave the parts of me

that are useful, the parts of me

that make my life worth living.

I have given my share of kindling already.

THERE'S NOTHING LEFT FOR YOU HERE

Don't fall in love

with my caliginous heart,

for it is immeasurably deep,

chasmed by sorrow and haunted

by ghosts that saunter through

the chambers of my soul.

IN THE GLOAMING

Envelop me in your vignette of darkness.

Obnubilate the memory of who I was before you.

I was but a specter in the gloaming,

forever lost, forever roaming.

GLASS OF KINDNESS

Trust trickles down my throat like bleach,

and naturally, I don't swallow easily

for I have been burned before

in ways I do not remember,

and it grieves me to think

how I should have known better.

I let the ones I loved

hold the bottle to my throat.

I guzzled their deceit until I gagged,

regurgitated, then choked—

on their acidic lies, so sour on my tongue,

it was only after I tasted bile

that I had learned my lesson.

How can I trust again

when my esophagus has been burned?

When every glass of kindness looks the same

as the trust that made my insides churn?

How can I let another offer me a sip,

when the bitter taste of betrayal

is one that I could never forget?

GRUDGES ARE SACRED

They are the prayers that hang

between our lips, acidic;

burning flesh.

They are the covenants we make

to save ourselves, no matter the cost

when no one else will.

FROST FLOWERS

We yearn for memories of pain,

immortalized like ice crystals

forming in our veins, they cut us

like razors slicing tendons root to stem,

until our anguish seeps, ruptures, then expands.

We treasure these frozen moments, and miss them

as soon as we release a cold winter's breath,

like frost flowers on the forest floor

blooming before their tiny deaths.

GARDEN OF FLESH

Do you hear the sound of my crackling lungs blooming
in brutal shades of blue, beds of
wolfsbane tempting you to look closely at my
veins sprawling like vines in the gloom?

This is my body, my garden of flesh.

It is haunted. Ghosts mourn over my scars, like barren
patches of earth marred by malice, and I, the farmer who
would not stop digging, tilled the earth until muscle and
skin folded into one another like limestone in the soil, an
effort to reduce the acidity, for how could I grow
anything in a garden nourished in self-pity?

What could I grow in a place where petals fell under the
softest touch? Where leaves crumbled and roots
shriveled up to die because there was no love left to
grow inside? It was only until the blade was ripped from
my hands that I grew to understand, I had become a
disease, a grub in the garden, torpid and hungry.

MUSCA

CREATURE

Motherhood started as a gaping wound

between my legs, a steady stream

of blood, tissue, and stitches meant

to close me up, make me whole again.

I've become a mother twice now

and I'm still unsure if that wound will ever heal

despite the sutures, the pelvic floor therapy,

the belly bands or any other gimmick

that can be thought of to mold me back into place.

Why is our society so focused

on putting its mothers back together?

It's one thing to advocate for healing,

it's another to bombard a mother with

weight loss ads, "you'll snap back!"

or mommy makeovers courtesy

of a plastic surgeon and his scalpel.

A modern Frankenstein and his creature,

will he disown us, too?

Will any of that fix our wounds?

Will any of that make us 'whole' again?

And what is it that we're trying to fill

other than the grave of the woman we were

before we had children?

The woman who didn't realize

that there were stars in her eyes,

comets that traveled through galaxies

of endless possibilities.

The woman who didn't realize

what she wanted until it was too late,

still hoping to make her dreams come true

before falling into the great void of a black hole.

Will society let us grieve over her, too?

Burrowed Pride

It's pride that settles in—
a growth, bubbling
saturating in pus,
and I can't seem to prick it
before it ruptures my skin.

With every passing day
it grows, and I am afraid
what will happen if it consumes
my entire being?

Will I just be a mass
of malignancy threatening
everyone around me?

My heart hurts
and that's how I know
it's burrowed into my roots.

Silent Promise

Daughters: when you were but tiny seedlings, I cupped
you in the palms of my hands and prayed my womb
would fertilize and nourish you.

I prayed the bones that poked through my root systems
would not disturb you, that sharp edges would not
protrude or pierce your soft hearts like a scalpel carving
away the little fingers and toes I so often bring to my lips
and kiss in silent promise.

A promise that I would not pass onto you my trauma;
that I would wrap my wounds and let my pain scab over
in healing for you.

CRIMSON DRABBLE

When you were born I prayed milk would flow from my breast to your suckling lips like a river of gold, colostrum that would nourish and give you the glow of health, but all my body knew was how to bleed.

I knew what I was: a vessel of trauma brimming with heartache and loss, but babies need to feed, don't they? Would my anguish poison you, too?

I stroked your rosy cheeks, wiped the crimson dribble off your lips, and made a vow. I would not let you get lost in the undertow of our maternal inheritance, too.

LUMINESCENCE OF INNOCENCE

Sweet curls glow in the morning sunshine

like golden fields of wheat, and she is mine

at least for now.

How quickly will the years pass by?

Will I only remember the moments she cried

because I wasn't enough for her?

We all make choices.

I choose to remember the luminescence

of her innocence.

If I Could, I Would Give You The World

Warm milk trickles down her throat—
liquid gold, a nectar as smooth as blood.

Mother hoped she would
be strong; that she would be brave.

Mother prayed she would devour the hearts
of her enemies and latch upon their beating muscles,

As ravenously as gums
clamping down on her mother's breast.

Mother would endure all the cuts,
scrapes, and bruises If the world was what she wanted.

A promise that one day Mother would give it to her.

Mother would tear apart the world for her, too.

PIECE BY PIECE

I am afraid

there is a sickness growing inside of you,

one that I could never prevent; inherited.

One that will take you away from me,

piece by piece, curl by curl,

blonde strands falling to the floor

for roaches to chew as the rats

gnaw on your flesh—

Your mind

is a precious place, a space

I hope the darkest parts of this world,

my world, do not infect, still

I see the sickness growing,

black bile spilling forth from me,

coagulating into a shape I do not recognize,

a figure that eerily looks like me,

its face covered in baby teeth—

Am I too late?

Do we still have time?

I look at your skin, smooth and milky,

the light in your eyes still shine.

The vermin

have not tasted you yet.

Not yet.

      Not yet.

Melancholy Doll

your touch, so distant

riddled with frisson

my melancholy doll

you're not in a prison

I just want the world for you

even if it's small

your fingers trace walls

and I am left heart broken

at the sight of you.

MOTHERS DROWN FIRST

Body frigid, clothes sodden,

and I am holding you above water

as best I can.

I will never let your feet dip below

the crests of waves so long as

corpses float beneath the surface.

It's too late for me,

my skin a mottled mess of cesious flesh,

worms feasting on my skin.

I will hold you up as long as I can,

until I know your feet have reached

shore.

Silent Reverie, Hold Out Hope For Me

You cried that night,

prayed for me to come home

while the wildflowers had grown

between my bones, and I dreamed

of you smiling during eternal slumber,

your glowing skin sun kissed by summer.

I imagined you found me

resting there in silent reverie,

that you had stayed and found your own serenity,

how lovely we were laying hopelessly immersed

in a world where I had not decomposed

in the billow of stems and dirt.

In The Full Bloom

The barren womb of her forgotten husk,

quietly decays in the full bloom of wildflowers,

stems lilting as their petals dance

a corps de ballet of yellow, purple,

and pink, where the only sounds

to be heard are the hushed whispers

of the wind and the twiddling

of two stems between the thumbs of a son

braiding daisy wreath crowns

his tears glimmer in the golden hour

for the mother he did not know,

and were it not for her quiet company

he would be wandering alone.

To Death, I Plea

Envelop me in tendrils of darkness,

where shadows cradle all my hurt,

all my fears,

Where grief dances

in fever dreams of moon flowers

blooming on riverbeds of chasm and loss,

Where memories of starlight

shimmer and glisten on crystal lakes

where nightingales sing,

Where she and I

are together once more

just as mother and daughter should be.

WHERE FIREFLIES DANCE

I fear the woods—

the damp earth where

the soles of my feet have not crossed,

trellises of root systems reach out

like the gnarled hands of Death, and yet,

she runs, so I must follow.

She is my heart.

She is the source of my fears.

It is here where she thrives, in shadows where

devils watch and hungry wolves drool,

where she giggles and howls at the moon,

where the will-o'-wisps guide her to the fireflies

that dance, a place I do not yet know

but hope to understand.

ACKNOWLEDGMENTS

Writing is a solitary journey. It is lonely, though this need not always be the case. I am fortunate to know and befriend the following individuals, who without, this book would not exist.

To Ravven White, my publisher, and friend. As I write this, it has been exactly one year since *Lady of The House* was published. You've since written another poetry collection, your debut novel, and continue to dedicate yourself to supporting the authors in your growing publishing house. Look how far we've come in one year! Let's see what happens in the next one.

To Erin Al-Mehairi, my editor and new friend. Thank you for 'seeing' me, my vision for this collection, and our conversations on womanhood, motherhood, and trauma. Your guidance in the technical and creative aspects of the craft was instrumental in my continued growth as a poet. Both the collection and I are better for it.

Thank you to SueAnn Summers for your interior artwork and Mark McClish for your cover design. I fervently wish that readers and writers continue to support your artistic endeavors, as you possess a beautiful, impressive, irreplaceable talent that is uniquely your own.

To Shannon Stephan, my friend, and fellow poet. You were among the first to know my plans for this collection. Whenever I needed counsel or found myself in doubt, you were there. I treasure our friendship and am excited to watch and support you as you embark on a new chapter in writing.

Thank you to my husband, who keeps me all together when I cannot. And to my daughters, who inspire me to continue my path of healing and be the best mother I can be, thank you.

Finally, thank you, dear reader. If you have found yourself wandering in endless night, I hope you know there is still time. You needn't venture too far into the darkness.

Light is out there.

Hope still exists in this world.

Sincerely,
Grace R. Reynolds

About The Author

Grace R. Reynolds is a native of the great state of New Jersey, where she was first introduced to the eerie and strange thanks to local urban legends of a devil creeping through the Pine Barrens. Since then, her curiosity with things that go bump in the night bloomed into creative expression as a dark poet, horror, and thriller fiction writer.

When Grace is not writing she can be found dreaming up macabre scenarios inspired by the mundane realities of life. Her short fiction and poetry has been published by various presses, including Brigid's Gate Publishing, Creature Publishing, Dark Matter Magazine, Death Knell Press, and more. Her debut collection of horror poetry, "Lady of The House," was released in December 2021 by Curious Corvid Publishing.

Connect with Grace on Instagram and Twitter as @spillinggrace, or her website: www.spillinggrace.com.

ABOUT THE ARTISTS

SUEANN SUMMERS, *interior artwork*

SueAnn Summers is an illustrator, poet, and writer from upstate New York. Having discovered the magic of transformation through art and writing at a young age, her spark for creating bloomed into a full blown passion. SueAnn began selling her paintings in a gallery at 18 years old and has since studied various mediums, techniques, and styles to create unique works of art for her diverse clients. While serving in the USN Seabees, she painted a large mural of the Seabees Memorial, which still hangs today in Pearl Harbor, Hawaii. From small details painted on egg ornaments, stationery, and book cover art to full illustrations and wall art, it is clear to see the love in each piece of her work. With each creation she sends to its forever home, a piece of her heart will be attached.

To connect with SueAnn, find her on Instagram @the_musing_palette.

MARK MCCLISH, *cover design*

Mark Alexander McClish is Curious Corvid Publishing's design director. He is also a high school digital arts and design teacher, and a few other things in his spare time. He's not particularly Gothic himself, but he does delight in the spooky. Mark attended Freed Hardeman University, earning his bachelor's degree in Graphic Design and a minor in Chemistry. After graduation, he and his wife, Shelby, moved to Murfreesboro, Tennessee, and have lived there since. He is the author of the award winning novel, Adhara's Sonder, published in 2021 by Curious Corvid Publishing.

To connect with Mark, find him on Instagram at @markmakesart247

CPSIA information can be obtained
at www.ICGtesting.com
Printed in the USA
JSHW061821280323
39571JS00003B/169